The Opposite of Clairvoyance

The Opposite of Clairvoyance

GILLIAN WEGENER

sixteen rivers press

My thanks to the editors of the following publications, in which some of these poems first appeared: *americas review, Runes: A Review of Poetry, In the Grove, English Journal, Stanislaus Connections, The Cloud View Poets (Arctos Press), The Mad Poets' Review, Quercus Review, Apostrophe,* and *hardpan.*

Many thanks to the members of Sixteen Rivers Press; to David St. John and the Whitman writing group; to all the Licensed Fools, past and present; to Helen Wickes, Murray Silverstein, Stella Beratlis, Lee Herrick, and Lee Nicholson; to Gary Short, Barbara Ras, Jane Hirshfield, Pattiann Rogers, and David Bullen; to Michael Wickes for his beautiful photography; and thanks to my parents, Ken and Barbara Wegener, to my aunt, Roberta Wagner, for those first poems; and, of course, to Joe and Sophia.

Published by Sixteen Rivers Press
P.O. Box 640663
San Francisco, CA 94164-0663
www.sixteenrivers.org

Library of Congress Control Number: 2007906041
ISBN: 978-0-9767642-7-4

Cover and book design: David Bullen
Cover art: Michael Wickes
Author photo: Dee Hawksworth-Lutzow

for Joe

Contents

I

The Opposite of Clairvoyance   13

Listen—   15

In a Rapidly Expanding City   16

February   18

Phone Call at the Dissolution of a Marriage   19

Eight Qualifications to the Idea of Individuality   20

After bringing out some coffee   22

Faith, Perhaps   23

Meadowlark   24

The Strip Joint Is Open All Week   25

Aviary   26

Reflection   27

February's Birds   29

January's Poem   30

Idaho Highway   31

2

I Start Again with the Smallest Details   35

Point of Departure   37

Phone Call with Little Purpose   39

Dreaming of You 40

A Poem in Which I Contradict Myself 41

On Hearing the Missing Writer's Been Found 42

Scene at the Kabul Zoo 43

Mud Slide, Acapulco, 1997 44

[Exit, Pursued by a Bear] 45

3

Funderwoods 49

The Sign Reads . . . 50

Scene on Highway 99 52

Postcard from Jane 53

Coffee Break 54

Scheveningen 56

The Soul, Feeling Expansive, Masquerades as a Butterfly 57

Song 58

Growing Season 59

Bugle Air 60

Observance 61

Fine China, San Juan Bautista 62

Sixteen Flowers 64

4

Another Apocalyptic Sign 69

Still Life with Phone and Prayer 70

Poem for the Insects 71

There's nothing beautiful about Los Angeles 72

Sidelines *73*

Scene with Hawk and Squirrels *74*

Smoots & Dooley Architectural Salvage *76*

After she says she's never been in love, she says . . . *77*

This Morning the World Is Populated Primarily by Birds *78*

City of Richmond *80*

The Lord God Bird *81*

Park Scene *83*

Persimmon Tree *84*

Magda Tells a Story *85*

Perspective *86*

I

The Opposite of Clairvoyance

You feel like a fool,
not being able to spot the bird,
the little bird making all the noise
contained in the center of you.

When did the tree become such a maze?
When did leaves become this impenetrable?

It isn't what you thought, standing here
under the tired green and hoping
so hard it's like a knife inside you
peeling off the soft tissue of your lungs.

Look hard enough, you are supposed to see.
Think hard enough, you are supposed to understand.

No one talks about the cold pain when this doesn't happen.

A nail in the foot, and then
the tetanus shot to save you from the nail.

The little bird keeps shrieking—sounds broken—
and your hope is that winter will make plain the bird,

will knock the leaves from that tree with a fist
hard and merciless as God's
and make plain that crying bird.

Listen—

the sharp-shinned hawk's ragged voice
etches a pattern here from ice true north,

the sound of fork against frying pan,
of crumpled, burning paper.

Even the sky is worn-out
on the last night of November.

A mute wind, and this light turns
the sycamore wrought iron,

delicate tracery, art nouveau
under streetlight, neck bowed

slightly to the left of its shadow.
The sky's vague, then vanished, suddenly dark.

In one house, the radio spills
a traffic report. In another,

television has turned the long room
into a blue shell filled with underwater light.

In a Rapidly Expanding City

Driving through streets,
asphalt so new and black thoughts wander
into dank mines to rest.

Houses snapped together, blocky and bland,
coordinated colors, tinted windows
gaze blindly at the twin across the street.

Here, someone reads the mail addressed to Resident.

Dust flies between stuccoed walls, dragging its feathers.

No protection from the long blankness of day.
The new sidewalk ages and gaps.

The dog in the yard starves for honest green.

Lawns like tidy factory carpets,
and the requisite city tree, resigned,
leaves already withering.

Here, someone arranges spices on the rack:
mace, nutmeg, oregano. Makes a note to buy paprika.

With no common language, the houses
ally themselves to nothing.

The resident lines up a snow globe collection
on a windowsill, listens to a garage door open and shut.

On the corner, the dust spins itself a tower.

Inside, under ceilings tall as winter skies,
grow the ghosts of vanquished walnut trees.
Below them, foundations slowly crack and shift.

February

That whole month, her chief pleasure is filling small bottles with water
and tinting each with single, hanging drops of Schilling food coloring.
The way the drop loosens in the water, the way it unwinds
into a thread, into a cloud, and then gives itself to the larger body
makes her dizzy. She needs to see it over and over and over.
One day she is in love with vermilion. Another day, indigo.
One morning she just lets the baby cry, trying for a certain shade of rose.
She lines the bottles up on the windowsill above the sink,
where the sun comes in for an hour or so each morning
before it slides away over the house and a chill returns.
There, the jars of colored water catch the sun and claim it,
make it dance, make it into stained glass, her private cathedral
falling onto the sinkful of soap suds and a morning's worth of dishes.

Phone Call at the Dissolution of a Marriage

He calls, my old friend, while wandering in the dark moors
of his misery, sorrow balled in all his pockets, anger caked
on the soles of his shoes and caught in his wild hair. He asks
questions as if I had answers about love and betrayal and
the reasons she would leave a pair of sandals behind, but
not the bedside lamp and not the dictionary.

Under this kind of sorrow, telephone lines should grow heavier.
They should swell or sag or dip so close to the ground that birds
fly elsewhere, confused. Telephone poles across the country
should bow and snap under the weight of this grief, but

they don't. From his phone to mine, two thousand miles of poles
stand rooted into the solid earth, straight as days, unconscious
of burden, carrying the hard sadness of my friend to me, who
can do nothing but grip the phone tightly and listen while
birds flutter and perch on all the taut wires between us.

Eight Qualifications to the Idea of Individuality

i.
Each person crossing on the green light at the corner
of Post and Van Ness comes with a complete set of sorrows
so similar that the crossers confuse themselves with each other
when they see their reflections in the opposite window.

ii.
In the field, this blade of grass
and an infinity of identical others,
whispering.

iii.
She leaves the office on Friday and does not return.
(heart attack? boredom? suicide? amnesia?)
By Thursday, she is replaced by someone equally qualified.

iv.
An article announces that fingerprints were never reliable,
that my fingerprints may be just like yours.

v.
He writes stories, hopes to make himself immortal.
He knows this is futile, but turns the page, starts again.

vi.

It may be arrogance to believe yourself most important
—the squirrel chattering unheeded at the jay—
or it may be survival.

vii.

On the freeway, cars filled with people never met,
stories never heard, hatreds and loves never felt.
The moon orbits the earth each month and is still mystery.

viii.

In any town, there must be someone each of us could love.

After bringing out some coffee

                          she turns away,
and he thinks of the first time he saw her,
at a cousin's wedding, in a yellow dress.
She'd never worn mud boots then, never
even been on a farm. And now
she turns away and walks back toward the barn,
her mud boots making little sucking sounds
as she goes, and he thinks of the way
her hips looked as she danced in that yellow dress.
It's been a day of rain and sudden sun.
It's been a year of maybes and warmed-over coffee.
He turns and watches her go.

Faith, Perhaps

Afternoons, sometimes, nearing dusk,
there was a certain glow around the edges of the room.

The sun by then low on the other side of the house;
the glow could not be from the sun.

It was not from the unrisen moon.

Hue a little gold, but sometimes bluish,
sometimes refracting, like being inside a diamond.

Always silence like that locked inside a diamond.

She'd sit very still in the glow
as if expecting a certain bird to alight on her hand,

her pulse tapping softly in her upturned wrist.

She was patient and she loved the glow:
its whimsy, its inability to explain itself.

She didn't need explanations.
She was tired of talk.

Sitting within it was nearly
enough.

Meadowlark

the radio bleats only the same bad news
the flags of compassion have grown ragged
the live oak throws off thick golden clouds of pollen
no one wants to be where they are
there's a yellow-bodied bird on the fencepost
the phone rings in an empty room
the radio's news is inevitably permanent
lily of the valley bobs next to the driveway
the dream last night was better than the whole length of today
that bird is a meadowlark, you hear someone say, and
the pollen clouds are both beautiful and dangerous
the phone rings on, the strident nag
the lily of the valley waves little white flags of compassion
no one wants to be where they are, which is to say, here
the dream was of an ex-boyfriend just calling to say hello
the song of the meadowlark cuts through the radio news
cuts through so sharply, it almost makes you cry

The Strip Joint Is Open All Week

Wednesdays are slow days. No one drives out from the city
of rattling elevators to sit in these sticky chairs, so the dancing
is for the sticky, empty chairs, and for the bartender pouring bowls
of peanuts back into the jar. Thursdays are different.
The weekend starts early, and the faces of the college kids
turn ancient and craggy under blue and gold stage lights. They're boys
really, in rugby shirts, still smelling of their moms' detergent. But
Fridays the place fills out, people push against the bar. One
at a time the girls dance, this one in gold, that one in feathers,
feathers falling around her, drifting down to a damp palm.
Saturdays the world opens up and shimmies, falls over on
itself, forgets time and just dances, rhythm something
the body washes in, something the body exhales,
but Sundays are another story entirely. Loneliness
creeps in at the windows and takes a seat. A man sets down
his beer and forgets to drink. Another falls asleep
at the corner table. The slap-tap-slide of the dance is almost
beside the point. Monday comes on like a cold snap,
like a draft around the legs of tables and chairs and dancers.
And Tuesday, no one's favorite and no one's least favorite,
is easy. Only the attentive come on Tuesdays. They eat
the peanuts slowly and lick the salt from their fingers. The girls
dance—gold, feathers—carefully, listening to the music
for the first time all week and pretending the twinkle-lights
strung around the room are the most distant, uncharted stars.

Aviary

The black ibis
tilts his slender head
toward the pan of sacrificial mice.
His eye shifts
slightly with anticipation.
He lifts his wing, black
in sunlight, blacker
in shadow.

The mice in their pan
are strangely flat, as if each fine bone
had been carefully slipped from its casing
leaving pink noses, pink tails, white fur,
a costume for a child's pet.

The ibis's yellow eye shifts,
his wing folds down.
No urgency.
The point is not the hunt.
There is nothing here but time.

Reflection

So you have trouble shifting,
have trouble, are troubled,
you can't quite manage how to make the leap,
even if it is not a leap really, but just a step,
or not even that, maybe a sitting up rather
than a lying down. Yes, if you have trouble
because you imagined her face so differently,
and now she is in front of you and her hair
is not even close to the fine perfection
you carried in your mind, not the auburn
you had pictured, and her eyes are misaligned
but so slightly it's not worth mentioning. And
now she is in front of you, right here in front of you,
and you are married, and in the other room
of this house that you always thought would be
bigger and more rustic, in the other room, there is
a child whom you assumed would play the cello,
or at least the guitar, but mostly the kid
seems to stare out the window. The kid is a dreamer.
And that wasn't the plan. And you go off to work
every day and stare at yourself staring back at yourself
in the train window and are surprised because,
boy-oh-boy, is it hard to make the shift between
all that you imagined (you were a dreamer) and

all that really is, and could that really be you . . .
the guy with the tie and the crow's feet and the glasses
in which there is an even smaller reflection of you
staring back in disbelief.

February's Birds

Late afternoon: the shadow line of the house
already a long slant against the fence,

the fence gleaming in sunlight, washed to pale gold,
the color of invalid tea and invalid toast.

February is a long, long month.

But suddenly a bird lands on the rain gutter
above this window. The tick-tick of spry feet on metal.
And then he's joined by another. And a third.

And there they are, gray bird shadows on the fence,
bending and pecking, pushing around the muck
in hopes of a meal. Feet tapping and clicking,
long tails upright and bobbing.

The world to them is no mystery,
and they are mostly pleased with it.

Then two fly off. One leaps up, the other down,
and they are gone, hollow-boned and chattering.

The third stays a long while, hopping on spindle feet,
rattling the rain gutter, both shadow and bird,
a live weather vane, one eye glinting toward spring.

January's Poem

January's a month of naked sticks,
lichen-crusted and gray,
moss gone damp and soft as sponge.
Cold clings to the insides of coats, creeps
into boots marooned on the rug.
Fog funnels in through the chimney,
rattles the window locks, fashions itself
into sheets thin as puddle ice, and
exits under the door. January's cranky,
moody as witch dreams, now threatening
to dampen, chill, and freeze us all, now,
quite gently, offering the snapped twig
with its wild tinge of green.

Idaho Highway

It is not difficult to imagine those eyes
reflecting headlights, vacant
and startled in a frantic second.
It is not difficult to imagine swerving away,
the suck of breath, the tire shriek and
the heavy thud, metal against bone.
And after that, it is not difficult to imagine silence
filling the space again between the road
and the somber stars.

Days later, the deer lies on the side of the road,
half in the grass, half out,
ribcage arched like fingers above piano keys,
fluttering scraps of hide, a haze of flies,
the eyeless fractured head tipped toward the east,
the direction from which death came.

2

I Start Again with the Smallest Details

The scar, shaped like a conquered Baltic country,
reminds me of nothing, being so old, so familiar
it has become only topography, nothing
more meaningful than that, though
also nothing less. It is a rough terrain,
but mine, and I know the way in,
and also the way out, since the map can't be lost.

And there is the sound of knuckles on wood,
that quick superstitious rapping for luck, or
softer taps that want admittance,
hope inherent in either sound.

Though softer in reflection, the light is ordinary;
a net of white, intangible tulle, it fills space and is like
the light anywhere—supermarket, classroom,
kitchen, gravity of cloud cover. It is nothing
like the bright light of experience though, not
that sharp, that hot, or that unrelenting.

The scar I would miss if it were gone.

The light—turn it off. I've seen enough.

The sound of knuckles on wood—I keep knocking,
keep knocking, for luck or admittance,
I'm never sure which.

Point of Departure

tongue-tied, she sculpts little numbers, bits of alphabet

feels the language out in air gone thick and malleable

as clay or mud, as the breathiness of meringue

what she wants is control though she doesn't like to admit this

(not ladylike) what she wants is to name everything

petiole: stalk attaching leaf to stem

verso: left-hand page of manuscript

she invents names sometimes—or similes anyway

explaining and explaining, drafting new rules of order

like a morning of miserable phone calls, which is different from

the clean pain of a paper cut on the tongue

punctilio: a fine point of etiquette (ladylike)

she wants control—like the carpenter, not the architect

she wants the house to fit the cosmos buzzing inside her left hemisphere

she wants the baseboard to fit exactly the angle between floor and wall

no unexplained spaces, 90 degrees—there's a close miracle in that

the click click of wood fitting against wood, yes, like that

a pleasurable green—color of newborn aphids

she wants everything named and simple, everything simple

everything named with shapes that open up, willing to be understood

(she feels ridiculous wanting this, tongue-tied and green)

fortitude: the moment between this breath and, yes, the next one

Phone Call with Little Purpose

Always the click of teeth as she speaks,
the tap of the ice in the glass, the pause
just into the call, a long pause like
a fishing weight in the palm, expectant.
She's lighting her cigarette, fumbling a little,
and I listen to her breathe in, breathe out.
The sound of smoke against the receiver is hushed
and violent, conversation beside the point.
I'm distracted by the newspaper even as she describes
last night's dinner in detail, or is it tonight's? And
when the chat pauses and she turns to tell
someone where the car keys are, neither of us
remembers what we were saying: weather? kids?
food? war? work? Outside, a car pulls up and pulls
away, but no one's gotten in or out. *What was that?*
I don't know either. The stodgy goodbye
picks up its hat, determined to leave. *I'll let you go.*
I'll talk to you soon. Yes, let's talk soon.
I always let her hang up first, the dial tone's hum
as comforting as knowing the exact count
of minutes between this call and, oh lord, the next.

Dreaming of You

I expected you days and months and years ago.
What unmapped path have you taken?

Only occasionally do I imagine your voice,
calling for me after sleep.

There is so much to show you: night skies,
oceans, how the ball fits inside the glove.

The hollow of my neck is yours.
So too is the crook of my arm.

Sorrow digs in her heels, calls for backup,
sips coffee from a styrofoam cup.

What do I do with your names,
inscribed as they are on my bones?

Feet, hands, hair, ears, eyes like mine,
I forget and remember this does not exist.

There is so much I want to say.
My throat aches from this hard silencing.

A Poem in Which I Contradict Myself

Some days are empty of poems.
The air whirls around simply like air whirling,
birds do their bird activities with no ulterior motives,
the earth rotates around the sun
because that is what the earth does.

Specifically, just now, an ice cream truck
is tinkling past the house, and I am thinking
of the time when I was six and conned
the Good Humor man into giving me
an ice cream sandwich because he was old
and there were too many kids and
he couldn't remember
who had paid and who hadn't.
All those sticky hands reaching up.
His cap pushed back, handing out
whatever we yelled for and
receiving nothing in return.

The silly music rolls past and
is gone around a corner.
The corner is just a corner,
the silence now just silence.

On Hearing the Missing Writer's Been Found

The little flowers on the plum tree are already springing loose,
and someone who will always remember this day spots a body in the river.
The day dawns warm and stays warm, and it's all over the news.
The writer's been missing for a month already, and now
with spring writing its name on everything with sticky fingers, and
the air, pollen-heavy and in love with newness, and the little creamy flowers
springing loose to make way for light-greedy leaves, the writer's
been found, and he's being pulled from the edge of the river.
The workers wear waterproof boots and waterproof gloves,
and they taste pollen on their lips, even as they lift the writer from the water
with his useless eyes and his forlorn arms and
                              his bitten ears like no known seashells.
The water's still cold and the workers think of coffee and stamp their boots, one-
two, on the dock. It's spring now and they think of coffee and also of baseball.
The writer's been found, but the history of this scar and that are lost to the river.
Its already all over the news how he was missing and how he was found, though
no one mentions the sadness of all the stories
                              in his fine, salt-licked brain washed away,
just as no one notices how the air has gone so thick and golden and dense
that suddenly the birds have taken to simply floating.

Scene at the Kabul Zoo

The lion is one-eyed and lonely,
his hide a moth-eaten costume,
hip bones shifting tensely, reminding the keeper
of the wing bones of fabled angels.

Dusk is falling over Kabul's wintry zoo.
The lion paces his desert pen with its gray walls,
a little straw, a pan of water in one corner.
The fleas in the lion's mane are hungry.

A green tenderness has grown between lion and keeper,
similar to the tenderness between men with an ancient grudge.
The keeper never approaches on the lion's blind side.
The lion keeps his savannah dreams to himself.

On the edge of the city, bombs are falling.
The zoo shudders. A monkey sends up an ignorant scream.
The zebras have long since died.
The lion, with his soft teeth,
with his matted mane,
with his cracked paws,
with his soul set against the hard press of winter,
settles for the night.

In the iris of his lonely eye, a city on fire flickers.

Mud Slide, Acapulco, 1997

The coffin hung, half in the earth, half out,
unsure, unbalanced, naked as a tooth.

Below, the violent mud, color of coffee, thick
as anger and spit, bit into the earth, scraped itself

a new path, pushed through, took everything in its way.
Above, the gray rain kept falling, always

in thick sheets from the tarnished sky.
Everything changed shape, even what we thought unchangeable.

The earth, gone weak and soft as the dying, finally sighed,
loosed its grip, and the coffin, narrow end first, tipped,

slipped into the torrent, almost graceful,
a strange boat plunging in the furious flow

toward some other resting place we'd never find,
as if some temperamental god was saying *Not here . . .*

. . . Here.

❧

[Exit, Pursued by a Bear]

And so it is with us all . . .
we do our little duties:
water the plants, tend the dog,
return the calls, etcetera . . .
when the bear finally finds us.

He is hungry and indiscriminate.

Our attention is usually elsewhere.
The moon, though vapid, sets us longing

and the bear, though heavy, moves
toward us as if he were made only
of breath and inevitability.

He cannot be escaped or denied.

Once he arrives, no amount of cajoling
will convince him to turn away.
Offered a handful of berries, he is grateful
for both the berries and the hand.

The pursuit does not depend on time of day.
The bear may watch for a long while,

eyes glittering, before beginning his approach.
Now the choice is yours—run, dodging trees
both fallen and standing. Walk, slowly,
without hesitation. Or stand your ground.
He has poor eyesight, but a keen sense of smell.
Rest assured, traveler, the bear will find you.

3

Funderwoods

The woods are oaks and spread their woody fingers over us.
Paint peels on the aging signs, this one a toothy squirrel
holding up a paw: *You must be this tall to ride alone.*
The girl running the carousel is a madonna, that serene.
Tickets are ten for ten dollars and curl in the hand like a pet.
Music falls out of the smaller trees, splashes and evaporates.
You must be this tall to ride alone on the child-sized roller-coaster,
the tilt-a-whirl, on mini airplanes, on dervishing teacups hot to the touch.
The bumper cars are broken, heaped together in a junkyard pile, and
the painted eyes on the squirrel are the almost-blue of skim milk.
The boy running the roller-coaster can't stop looking at the carousel madonna
while her horses lift up and down, leather reins worn to brittle strips.
The airplanes have names like Thunderbird and Thundercloud, and
there's no waiting in line here. Two kids on that ride, one on this.
Under the roller-coaster, weeds with feathery leaves bend and flower.
Music falls out of trees and into our laps, a little sticky, a little cool.
The rides click and whir, creak to stops, jolt to starts.
The oaks spread their woody fingers and pattern the pavement.
The roller-coaster boy has left his post and whispers his plans
into the carousel girl's benevolent ear. She smiles, still serene, and
takes the curled ticket of a child who runs to find the perfect horse,
who cannot imagine a more shining moment than this.

The Sign Reads: *Area closed*
to protect natural features and insure public safety
Do Not Enter

the little convolvulus with their soft pink throats
make their way in any fine dirt, unbothered by thirst,
made for thirst, the funnel-flowers, the velvet leaves
all for collection   Queen Anne's lace, first-named
flower, grows obligingly by the road, her little halo
of buds pressed closed   waiting
here, so many things I don't have names for—
the spiders with their pithy nests shaped like tornadoes,
the nuts on the ground, meat scavenged out, gaps
where the meat's gone tapered, like thoughts before sleeping
where dreams edge in eager fingertips to rub
the back of your neck   and everywhere blackberries
the ruby half-ripe ones and the perfect, purple fat ones and
the hard, new green ones, sharp and bitter, almost without promise
blackberry juice pooled on the tongue is a precious little lake
of August   and with no thought of safety, the vines,
all thorns and sticky runners, make their way
to all the high places—sapling tops and fence rails and
sunny rocks leading down to the water   where fish
hang suspended like ornaments, hardly moving   who knows
if a fish is patient—the perfect water bug
always comes along   and there is a trick

in the numbers—each fish has its body, brown and tight,
to contain it, and each fish has its shadow, brown
and shimmering against the rippled bottom   the eye wants
a creek full of fish and gets it   and a duck too
with her brown body all purpose and pluck as she
swims upstream scattering the fish, tail feathers
the heated blue of kings and newly dark skies   a fly
lands in a funnel web, struggles a little, moves a veined wing
the light shifts   a new leaf catches the sun and
goes white with it   everywhere
an endless entering in

Scene on Highway 99

Disneyland is two hundred miles gone and the sun,
trailing its dusty skirt, is just beginning to set
long trails of crows pump through the pinking sky,
leaving the ironwoods with their silvery bark every night
to follow the highway north and north and
even as the traffic below them slows they don't look
down and don't look back, they know what they know
they've seen it before, brake lights in long rows
like runway lights and people reaching to adjust the radio
to some local station for an explanation found
all too soon there's the red splash-blue splash of lights
against the window and then the flares and then the scene
of the accident—burnt oleander smells like creosote—
and the car's still smoldering too and no one should look and
everyone does and there are the police measuring lines of trajectory,
the firemen hosing down the spilled gasoline, and the car,
no one wants to believe they will crumple like that, being winched
onto the tow truck breath held and held and suddenly the sky's dark,
the oleanders bounce like cheerleaders as traffic picks up and the crows
in their black coats have landed on the roofs of stores all over town
calling to each other in a language made of broken glass.

Postcard from Jane

Beautiful is too small a word for Yosemite.
I haven't been here in years
and the girls,
contained in their soft, new lives,
have never seen anything like it.

The baby laughed at the tramping
of our feet on the gravel path.

Emma said the falls are like wild horses.
Her pockets are full of smooth little stones.
I wish you could see the meadow—
how green is so many different colors.

We are coming home tonight.
The moon, our old friend, is almost full.

Coffee Break

God stops at Latif's for a cup of coffee and a piece of pie.
The orange vinyl of the booth creaks a little under his weight.
The circle of coffee in the cup is the exact opposite of the moon
and both are reflected in the eye of God as he looks at them.
The waitress taps the pencil against her order pad.
God cannot decide on which pie to have.
The apricot is good, but so is the coconut cream.
The waitress says, "I'll give you another minute,"
but what is a minute to God? He orders the coconut cream.
God admires the fine order of the rows of booths,
the way the scrubbed high chairs stand at attention in the corner,
and all the coffee cups, tucked into their tray upside down,
anticipating the morning rush with its usual scent of bacon.
God sighs in satisfaction and looks around to speak, but no one's listening.
At the counter, the busboy is filling salt shakers.
Across the aisle a group of farmers linger over coffee,
speaking the sensual language of weather and rootstocks.
God glances at the sky: rain over the weekend, but no frost.
The waitress brings the pie, refills the coffee. (God does not drink decaf.)
God eats and thinks, if he had to do it over again, pie
would play a more important role in the way of all things.
How can you not like pie, thinks God, licking meringue from the fork.
The farmers' fingers are rough and gnarled as olive branches,
the waitress's shoes squeak on the linoleum when she turns.

God contemplates the goodness of this particular moment
and is happy, but he has to move on. He leaves his money
on the table under his coffee cup. The waitress is pleased.
God, it turns out, is a mighty good tipper.

Scheveningen

The North Sea is not too cold for the swimmers waving back to shore.
We buy a pail, a shovel, and a bright red sieve at the corner shop.
A day shot through with sun and wind—built up with blue air and feathers,
the broad smell of the sea and new herring, which is the taste of the sea.
The seaside carousel is closed until two; horses under the striped cover, deaf.
Seagulls beating back the wind; the wind biting back with sharp little teeth.
Our small girl licks her melting ice cream and says *It tastes like kites.*
On the boardwalk, people lounge behind windbreaks, browned and drowsy.
In the red sieve, seashells clatter and scrape. Sand falls through like sugar.
She leans in and tastes her dad's ice cream and says *It tastes like sun.*
The old hotel sits up straight behind the bathers and sunners like a Victorian *oma.*
See where the ocean floor drops, where the water changes from blue to gray?
And when our girl, with sand in her eyelashes, tastes my cone: *It tastes like umbrellas.*
An old man, dressed smartly in his tweeds and cap, nods, but doesn't smile.
In the red sieve the clean seashells wait to become windows on today's castles.
Like a Victorian *oma*, all petticoat and parasol, a bit strict, a little indulgent.
The water changes from blue to gray all at once. The clouds have no favorite.
He doesn't smile at us, but he smiles at our girl, hands resting on his cane
as she runs ahead toward the sandy carousel, pockets full of seashells,
hands sticky with this kite-flavored day.

The Soul, Feeling Expansive, Masquerades as a Butterfly

Attaching the wings is the easy part.
A dab of glue here and here, and stretch.
See how the light comes through, pinks the air,
drops a sudden pattern on the sidewalk.
Next the furred mask, the antennae like breathy threads,
and adjusting them just so in a mirror
made of puddle and sky.

The soul anticipates flight as if it were not imagining,
tastes the air, tests the wind, flutters
the veined wings, feels the small whir
in the center of itself, that engine of yen and excitement.

The daylight shifts and shifts back,
breath and magic and breath,
a world gone keen with glint and shine.
The air tastes like lemon and the secret mouths of penstemon.

The soul scans the whole wide view,
lifts the costume wings and jumps,
both feet at once, into a horizon
as open as the beginning of a story.

Song

Each summer the wild birds shed their songs like feathers,
molt them into reeds and shadows.
The songs decompose, give themselves up to earth.
Earthworms pause to listen.
Hades hears, inhales the audible longing. Above,
summer birds, turning silent as monks, observe the lengthening days.

In fall, they'll build their songs again. A melody, note on note,
 a new voice, a trill to flutter against the cold,
call the mate, build the nest, herald the chicks,
defend the nest, welcome the scrubbed and shining spring,
the world wiped clean, the world entirely rewritten.

Growing Season

Our girl, newly hatched from her cocoon
of clothes, runs circles in the grass, laughing,
her skin smooth and glee-ridden, our garden nymph.
Her father waters the camellias with all their
slick new leaves, and when our girl runs close
he sprinkles her legs, and she runs shrieking
Don't water me! Don't water me!, but circles
toward and away from the sprinkling until
she is soaked, head to toe, and the jays look down
from their telephone wires to see her laughing.
Even the hummingbird stills to listen. And I
stand at the doorway with a towel pressed between
my hands, and I want to shout *No* and *Stop* and *Wait,*
and I say *No* under my breath, and *Stop,* and *Wait,* unheard
and helpless to slow this steady fling of days.

Bugle Air

Someone gives the kids a flea-market bugle.
They push their breaths through hard.
Cheeks hurt. Veins throb in young necks.
The harsh *pwaaahhhh* is a tongue stuck out
then pulled back, again the polite child.
Oh joy and pain, oh petal-tender night.
Plum faces darken with unabashed strain.
When one comes up gasping, the others
grab for the instrument with grubby hands.
Everyone wants to play, even if it hurts.
Everyone wants the air to tremble at their least bidding.

Observance

Across the street a man is dying.
His friends keep coming to visit in their large cars.
They hesitate before slamming the doors shut.
They think the noise might disturb him, or
the noise is too much like end punctuation
in the sentence of his life, or
they really just want to get back
in their large cars and drive away again,
have a picnic, pretend the sick friend is fine,
pretend we are all immortal.

Fine China, San Juan Bautista

When customers come in there's always a game on the radio.

A bell rings at the door. The man behind the register looks up.

All around him china gleams the color of sunlit bones.

Right now it's baseball, another couple months, football.

He looks up, but doesn't smile, avoids eye contact.

He loves the china, the whiteness of it, the smoothness.

This in a town known for earthquakes and its Spanish mission.

The customers make him nervous, so he tries not to watch.

China on shelves from floor to ceiling in order of issue.

Signs tacked up at eye level on each shelf as warnings.

Tries not to watch the fat woman with the large purse.

Plates stacked no higher than twelve. Cups stacked in fours.

Sometimes he holds a plate up to the light.

Take Care! Delicate! Haviland China! on yellowing paper.

How the purse swings from her shoulder unheeded, unwieldy.

The odd relish dish companion to the odd saltcellar.

When the crowd at the game cheers, it's startling.

He can see his hand behind the plate, as if encased in shell.

He wants to thank the parents who do not bring in their children.

The last big earthquake closed the highway for days.

It's this shop filled with light and held breath.

He prefers the plain china to the intricate.

The quake before that crumbled adobe walls at the Mission.

It's startling, as if cheering might set the earth in motion.

He thinks gaudy patterns betray the china somehow.
Sometimes he isn't sure if he loves the place, but
when the next earthquake comes, this is where he wants to be.

Sixteen Flowers

Hsu Wei came to painting late in life,
stunned by the sound of brush on paper.

The ink could hold a line or become a cloud,
could etch the begonia or shade the leaves around it.

After his time as a bureaucrat, he craved only
the unmarked scroll, clean brushes, fresh ink.

Bamboo in the background, rocks in the foreground,
calligraphy falling and falling like rain.

Winter blossoms alongside summer blossoms,
the blessing of everything at once.

Nothing in the scroll speaks of suicide—
his attempt, his failure, his continuing on.

Imagine the joy of the narcissus—
eternal beauty for the beloved image.

The dance life of the peony:
dip, brush, another sweep of delicate ink.

Seven years in jail for the murder of his wife.
Which is she in this spill of flowers?

The camellia's fragility—if the scroll wavered
in any breeze, the petals would fall and scatter.

First a playwright, Hsu Wei knew the staging
for each flower, each leaf, each stem.

The thick petals of the lotus would turn palest pink
without the slightest hesitation.

How did the light fall through the doorway as he worked?
What slant? What color? What shadows?

He loved the calligraphy, its look on the paper,
footprints in new snow.

Spring blossoms alongside autumn blossoms,
the curse of everything at once.

Hsu Wei never meant for the flowers to last.
Beauty fades, he mourned, and went on painting.

4

Another Apocalyptic Sign

The sign reads *Jesus Is Coming Quickly*
and I imagine Jesus coming on the run
down the main street at rush hour.
He's never learned to drive, so there he is
with his robes flapping behind him, his feet
beating the hot pavement, unsandaled and wounded.
He wears no watch, but has somewhere
to be and is already later than he'd like.
See that little furrow of worry between his eyes?
Drivers don't know what to make of him.
He doesn't bother with sidewalks or bike paths,
so there is some swerving in and out of traffic.
Brake lights slam and flash. Someone honks.
Most folks think he's just another crazy, but
they'll realize their mistake soon enough.
After all, there must be a reason Jesus is coming
quickly to this town, at this moment, charging
across the intersection even before the light turns green.

Still Life with Phone and Prayer

She would sit perfectly still
though the leaves outside shivered
and the clouds could not be contained
and the train pushed past and its whistle
threw itself into trees and scattered.
She would sit perfectly still,
the phone a grim statue of itself
arranged just so on the corner of the desk,
a little black shrine to wanting,
the dust around it part of the tableau,
everything tensed for the not-ringing.
Stillness of girl, stillness of phone,
(no rose, no fruit, no opened bottle,
no gentle light, no pewter cup),
just girl and phone and now
her thousand unstilled prayers
flung into the blue air and
fluttering like so many new-hatched,
light-addled moths.

Poem for the Insects

We winced at each chitinous clack against the windshield,
blinked against the certainty of the end of another small winged being.
The yellow-green smear of insect bile washed away easily enough,
but that washing away was no form of forgiveness.
Only the butterflies left a small gift, their wing glitter on glass—
a shimmer that would last for miles, then evaporate.
I dreamed an entire sky of butterfly glitter, but
a dream is no truth, and truth was blue in the morning
and a cantankerous gray most afternoons.
Insect after insect flew its kamikaze mission and succeeded.
Our car became a patchwork of legs and wings and body fluid markings—
a rolling insect-eliminator, no discretion, no favorites;
we took whatever came our way, a single june bug,
a horde of yellow moths, and the one we found nearly intact,
the grasshopper, orange and black stripes, with his head stuck
between the wiper blades as if he were looking for a missing friend.
His circus legs dangled, a bizarre and headless marionette.
We couldn't protect them, couldn't go over or under, just through.
The world a cloud of insect humming and insect bodies
and us speeding along inside it, cruel intruder, meeting it head on.
We didn't mean to be cruel, but all we could do was cheer
for each lucky bug that didn't hit, that caught the updraft,
that flew over us, and won a chance salvation.

There's nothing beautiful about Los Angeles

                        except
the *curandera*'s neon hand
looming out of the briny night,
the lines of her palm pulsing,
offering a reading, a remedy,
some affordable comfort
to the blank-eyed drivers
crawling past on the freeway.
It's 11:15 on a Friday night
and they're all heading southward
toward Hollywood, San Diego,
Tijuana, or some other
magic kingdom of the mind.
There's nothing beautiful in Los Angeles,
except this hand
and the sudden way the moon
sneaks in, tipsy and orange,
balancing just so
on the thumb's neon tip
before sliding off
and becoming
just another
streetlight.

Sidelines

Look at that couple in the corner.
It must be her birthday, prim thing,
sitting with her hands folded in her lap,
neat drink in front of her, ice splitting
in it and then splitting again, a mild cracking.
Look at the boy, see how his eyes wander.
Duty, that curmudgeon, is what brought him here.
The boy longs for popcorn and adventure,
for a girl who would unfold her hands and dance,
for the shouts of a rowdy friends, but mostly
he wishes the girl would just finish her drink,
that this little tableau would just end.

Scene with Hawk and Squirrels

She didn't like my spying.
I was greedy and wanted a look,
knew there was a nest up there,
ugly chicks inside it—all gaunt and unfeathered.
Just one little look, but she said *no*.
I did not speak her language, but I knew this.
The squirrels knew it too, chattered and scurried.
No is the same, regardless of species.
I acquiesced, I gave in, I shuffled on,
shoes tromping up dust, head down.
I know when to be humble, but she,
mean little eyes made of vinegar and filigree,
would have none of that. Down she came.
It is not enough to say *down she came*.
She dropped, wings back, neck stretched—
you've seen this in cartoons.
I felt her wing thud; the air went stiff with it.
Just above me, she tipped her wings and rose.
The air treated her gently, and she perched
in a live oak, screaming myths and obscenities,
her displeasure, a nails-on-chalkboard resonance.
All this happened three times. After the first,
the gray squirrels froze and then disappeared.
After the second, I crouched low to the grass,

imagining talons in my hair, considering hats.
For the third, I had a running start,
made it to the car, watched her coast around,
languid, satisfied, and perch again, eyeing me,
my birder's heart a little frantic, fingertips prickling.
That day the sky became bluer and smaller, while underground,
the squirrels cleaned their thrifty paws and waited out the drill.

Smoots & Dooley Architectural Salvage

The box of glass doorknobs. The box of hinges. The box of sturdy screws.

The iron gates to a hundred different gardens—now a hundred gateless gardens.

Everything's homeless here, singular and naked. Limbs without bodies.

Doors lean like tired men against the long wall, knobless and patient.

Window frames divide the world into quarters or eighths and miss their old views.

All these wrought-iron flourishes and curlicues, the alluring texture of rust.

Paint peels into little curls of faded blue and yellow. Even white can fade.

In a chipped enamel bowl set on a stove with no oven door, a cat sleeps.

Everything's homeless, bodiless, so many mix-and-match puzzle pieces on display.

Commodes lined up so daintily they can only be called commodes.

The box of glass doorknobs catches the light and breaks it into a million pieces.

Even white fades, becoming less and less itself, becoming a thin wipe of dust.

Texture of rust, flaky, gritty, that metallic smell, that dangerous color.

Does the window know its housemates? Would the door recognize its hinge?

The old views over the gardens, the plumbago near the painted gate.

The paint peels and falls, yellow and blue doll curls, sharp and sad.

The screws, long as fingers, thick as fingers, clack and murmur to each other.

One gate has a key stuck in the lock, too stubborn to give up on purpose.

How much for this hinge, these screws? How much for each doorknob?

The bowl has a blue rim. The commodes are so white, they glare and stun.

I'll take the entire box of knobs if they'll get me through each and every door.

After she says she's never been in love, she says . . .

I stay married because I meant what I said—
for better or worse, richer or poorer, sickness or health.
You can't take those words lightly, and a promise is a promise
even when it comes out worse and poorer and more sickly
than you'd hoped. Besides, he loves me and there's no one else
to do for him if I don't. He's a good man, just lost in the world.
I'm fond of him too, I guess, the cuss.
Some days, I'd even call it love.

This Morning the World Is Populated Primarily by Birds

Crows claim the sidewalks
and imitate humans, walking
in twos and threes, nodding
in their widow's weeds
and their shiny black suits.

Upstart starlings rule the schoolyard,
move across the soccer field
like soldiers in formation,
pecking in the grass for loot.
Each lifted head flashes green,
each yellow eye flashes menace.

Magpies fly low
down the center of the street.
The black and white and blue of them,
stark against the morning,
an ink drawing.

And jays, blue hoodlums, steal
the early strawberries, still hard and green,
and eat them standing in the driveway,
heads up and proud, gullets open.

There are fat robins too, and sparrows
in their plain brown wrappers,
and some yellow-headed bird,
a warbler maybe, hunched in the myrtle
like a stowaway.

One hummingbird, territorial brat,
chirps angrily at another. The smaller one,
the intruder, sweeps off loftily,
a blur of arrogance and feathers.
He'll bide his time a bit,
come back later.

City of Richmond

A river splits it, serrated water, a few barges.

Fireflies along the edges of parking lots, like runway lights.

Vertigo from looking up at Jefferson Davis.

The museum guard shouts in a room full of swords, "The war ain't over yet!"

The water in the river is the color of tobacco spit.

The vines spring up flamboyant, waving little kerchiefs the texture of damask,

not the rattley brown of California.

After work hours, the abandoned city doesn't feel like entertaining.

Burning oil, honeysuckle, the scent of rain soon.

The river holds itself still, on the river the shadows of clouds,

pinkish smoke makes its way delicately among the barges.

Grits heavy on the plate, like a city in the process of melting.

Antebellum houses ache and fail, paint peeling back like Bible pages.

Jefferson Davis's monument swills in humidity, his sword is chipped.

It's like breathing someone else's breath, someone you don't love.

After work hours, the city dresses down, buses run backward or not at all.

At the Canal Walk, groups of black people, separate groups of white people.

More monuments: Jackson, Beaumont, Lee, Fighting Joe Hooker.

The edges of the city are being consumed quite thoroughly by vines.

Like someone you don't love, but maybe could get used to.

At the end of the street of Civil War monuments, a marble Arthur Ashe.

The pale-haired bouncer slaps bat in hand, wooden *smat smat*, checks IDs.

In the abandoned city, after work hours, a tourist turns a map over and squints.

Even the green beans taste like cigarette smoke, but not in a bad way.

He can't read the map. The streetlights keep flashing out.

❧

The Lord God Bird

"a creature that does and does not exist"

This bird is the ghost that rumors the forest,
sets teeth on edge, moves the heart to achy greed.
The best binoculars are not enough to make it appear
out of the dense canopy of the favored swamp trees.
Just a look. Just a look, craves the birder's soul.

In field guides, the bird is noted briefly, if at all,
under the agnostic heading, *Probably Extinct.*
But we keep looking, the early sun shining
through the branches, air breathy with mosquitoes,
ground livid with snakes. The sun falls down
through the fat leaves accidentally and gets lost in spiderwebs
and dark bayous. We walk for hours.

There is bookish evidence: a photo, a yellowed journal entry,
Audubon's delicate thrill of a painting, even a recording—
the singular, nasal voice bleating a nagging reminder of loss.
But this does not satisfy. This is not what we want.

We want the bird itself. We want the bird here on a low branch,
black feathers and white ones neat on the long, warm body.
We want the crimson top crest and the yellow angry eye,
and the spectacular bill most of all, with its lunar luster,

beautiful and dangerous, the unlikely paleness flashing in the sun
as the bird leaves the branch and flies over us, alighting again
in plain view, where it sees us and doesn't seem to mind.

But what we get is a forest of wandering, a neck that aches
from gazing skyward, and untrustworthy ears that keep hearing,
in the distance, the flap of wings and the pierce of wide-open birdsong.

Park Scene

It is July, and the heat is trite, but makes good small talk.
A girl at the corner is reading a paperback with yellowed pages.
In the playground, my daughter plays hard, not minding the heat.
The girl, maybe nineteen, holds the book up to her face like a mirror.
She doesn't mind the blizzard of wooly aphids, this year's infestation.
The heat lies down, uninvited and heavy, on top of us all.
That girl, I think, does not notice wooly aphids or heat. She waits
for the light to turn. She has her back to us, but her hair
is the auburn of movie stars, that heavy, that thick. It has its own heat.
What book is she reading? The pages flutter a little and then don't.
The heat is the same old thing, but gives us something to chat about.
Her hair curls down her back just so, and she wears a black dress.
The girl knows she is beautiful, knows people are watching.
My daughter wants to come down the slide, but the slide is too hot.
The black dress is short and somehow gauzy; she's a delicate witch and
her legs are the smoothest white. She doesn't care about tans.
The slide is too hot, but the swings are in shade. We never see her face.
Just the black and the auburn and the heat, and no, she would never
notice wooly aphids, not even if they were falling like snow
into the pages of her book. She wouldn't even notice if the heat
were suddenly to lift, leaving us moms pushing our children
in the creaky swings, wondering what we were talking about.

Persimmon Tree

And after the last leaf is gone
from the cosmos of its branches,
the persimmon stands naked,
exposed, arms open and in a mood
for giving. On this tree
a hundred hearts are offered
for your pleasure, each red-orange,
each smooth to the hand. Take them.
You have your bushel basket.
Pick each one and hold it in both hands
for just a second before dropping
it in with the others. This way
you'll know to use all you take.
When you are done, there will
still be some left, too high to reach.
This is the way of the persimmon.
It will keep a few for the crows,
a few for the traveler,
a few for the cosmos
of its own stark body.

Magda Tells a Story

One night, snow light as ash flies,
we left the restaurant with friends, all
full of dolmas and wine, roasted tomatoes,
pickled cauliflower, light from the market next door
slapping a chill rectangle onto the grave parking lot.
Everything was shadow and brightness, the world
gone black and white and blurry,
the trees thick and bald with winter.
Who spotted them first? The little birds
balled into fists at the ends of branches,
heads drawn down into their bodies.
We could have reached up and touched them,
but didn't. Night birds, winter birds,
cold little ornaments on the tree of the new year.

Perspective

At some point the valley opened.
It started from a small point, then several, an ellipsis.
It opened from there like a museum of itself,
self-conscious, artifacts out, a little glossy. She, visiting—
For a while it was like this, then something happened:
a book fell open, an orchard of apricots unfolded,
no museum here. People live in the broad wind,
know the seasons of walnuts, the names of waterways,
San Joaquin yes Mokelumne yes Stanislaus yes.
Alkali lakes, and still that tree line means water
maybe so far down that the earth above it jigsaw cracks.
Eucalyptus can suck the saltwater from the ground,
thus saving the field. *Food grows where water flows* amen.
Signs up and down the open valley, hung from old freight cars.
Is it easier to grow cotton or almonds? Either way
it takes twenty-six hours to irrigate a field that size. Sleep an hour
here or there, water on the field like a mirror for God.
The valley opened from a small point and grew bigger, a tattoo
of sorts; she knew it would never leave her now.
A yellow-headed blackbird and two rows of palm trees,
the sky a cupped palm above the valley.
She under the palm and not claustrophobic.
May through December, gold hills like rick-rack.
Wild oats aren't native to the valley, but took over.

Not in a mean way; everything just wants to survive.

The eucalyptus aren't native, neither are table grapes.

The native tules have seen their clattering numbers dwindle.

First ranches, now houses, earth underneath groaning with the load.

If it weren't for wild oats, the hills would be grayish-green all summer.

The oaks would still be there but on a gray-green canvas.

At some point the valley opened and let her in for good.

She wasn't expecting this, but it seems right.

She won't say she wasn't hoping.

Notes

"Phone Call at the Dissolution of a Marriage" is for T. D. J.

The title "*[Exit, Pursued by a Bear]*" is from act 3, scene 3 of Shake-speare's *The Winter's Tale.* The poem originally appeared in *English Journal* and is reprinted with permission. Copyright 2004 by the National Council of Teachers of English.

"Postcard from Jane" is for the Cluff family.

Latif's coffee shop, mentioned in "Coffee Break," is located in Turlock, California.

"Scheveningen" is for my daughter, Sophia. Scheveningen is a beach on the Netherlands coast in The Hague.

The ink-on-paper scroll *Sixteen Flowers* currently hangs in the Philadelphia Museum of Art. The artist, Hsu Wei, lived in China from 1521 to 1593.

The poem "The Lord God Bird" owes much, including the epigraph, to the article "The Ghost Bird," by Jonathan Rosen, which appeared in the May 14, 2001, issue of *The New Yorker.*

GILLIAN WEGENER has had poems published in numerous journals, including *Runes*, *English Journal*, *americas review*, and *In the Grove*. A chapbook, *Lifting One Foot, Lifting the Other* was published by In the Grove Press in 2001, and she was awarded a top prize by the Dorothy Sargent Rosenberg Foundation for 2006. Wegener works as a junior high English teacher in California's Central Valley. She lives with her husband and daughter in Modesto.